Rain Following

Rain Following

Poems

Sue Lenier

THE OLEANDER PRESS

OLEANDER MODERN POETS XIII

The Oleander Press
17 Stansgate Avenue
Cambridge CB2 2QZ, England

The Oleander Press
210 Fifth Avenue
New York, N.Y. 10010, U.S.A.

British Library Cataloguing in Publication Data

Lenier, Susan Jennifer
　　Rain following.—(Oleander modern poets; 13)
　　I. Title II. Series
　　821'.914　　　PR6062.E 5 /
　　ISBN　0-906672-19-8
　　　　　　0-906672-20-1 Pbk

Typeset, printed and bound in Great Britain

CONTENTS

Somewhere inside me there is a scream . . . a building, tottering, skyscraper scream—a scream that, at night-time, lies and rustles and never leaves me alone to sleep. I have forgotten Sleep. I have forgotten his face and the blinding haziness of his mind and warm, woollen arms wrapping me round like a baby and rocking, cradling me in his arms. Call back Sleep to me . . . I have forgotten him . . . I have forgotten his face.

Do you know I move all the time? Endless movement, endless and pointless, I walk not knowing where I am going. When I get there, I cannot stop, I turn around and walk back again. Sometimes when the sun is high and golden, and people are lying on the grass, warm and golden asleep in the sun, I look upwards and think about waiting, think about stopping but then the sun starts to tick loudly again in my ears and the sky goes off like an alarm and I start walking quickly onwards again, never knowing where I'm going but onwards, onwards and I feel the scream rush backwards into my mouth and I hurry off back into the dark and a night where I cannot sleep.

(*Dancer* and *Instructor*. Written to be performed to Chopin's
Nocturne in D Flat Major)

D. . . . Is melting slowly, fog is melting slowly

I. Lift, twist out and turn.

D. The rain is singing

I. Raise your arms then gently lay them down.

D. Rain is singing, listen rain is singing

I. Legs

D. In bitter tears

I. Swing slowly to the side
Now swing them and lift

D. And bitter tears are running like a child's dark eyes
Autumn winds mock tumbling as birds fly dead through the rain
Simplicity lies mumbling and swallows
Fly, sweep away and freeze. Tints of autumn
Rain shining blues, greens, fly to the sky

I. Down

D. Pretty tears black wet sweeping black wet
Where the swallows fly

I. Up.

D. See them fly

I. Legs swing around and down—aside
Legs swing around and down

D. Red comes, green comes, autumn

I. Down

D. Red, green, brown.

I. Swing

D. Fly pretty

I. To the side . . . Lift . . . Point . . . Arabesque

D. Falling sky

I. Stretch your legs and graceful bring them down

D. Flying high, flying high.

I. Point

D. Falling sky

I. And point

D. See the swallows fly like tears
Like tears are flying from a child's dark eyes.

I. Arabesque. Arabesque
And point and flicking lift your eyes
Oh eyes straight
Head up. Now your

D. Late. The fog lifts

I. Head must be

D. Curved to the wind

I. Head must be down. Legs

D. Bleak like leaves
As they swoon with

I. Music

D. Brown and late
  Soft and

I. Straight.

D. Breath.

I. Hold.

D. Late. Dancers swirl in curving ever death.

I. Fall out and kneel
  See the dancers pall

D. Let us mourn

I. The dancers graceful fall

D. Let us mourn, let us mourn
  See the twinkling of the leaves
  Death. Death.
  The swallows sleep in soft black sheaves
  Raindrops skip in glittering silver lines down empty parades
  Made soft in signs of shades of grey that startled fades
  Draping autumn's glory parade

I. Sway

D. Sweet scent

I. Away . . . swing . . . rest

D. Arab . . . arab . . . arabesque.

I. Follow, follow, follow, follow, follow
  Singing arms in lines like flowers

D. Swallow swallow swallow swallow swallow
   Pretty swallows fly away

   Singing arms in lines like flowers
   Pretty swallows fly away
   Swinging arms in lines like flowers
   Pretty swallows fly away

   Pretty swallows stray in lines like flowers that fade away.

I. And rest.

▽

A child has slung her colours on the world
And left it blue. The faint cold dew
Of rose-born early winters litter the streets
With icicle fingers and promises tasting of snow,
You are wild and you have painted the sky
A new and an ivory hue. Looking upwards
Far in the early gold, I pick the ivory longingly
Pick it and kiss it, thinking of you.

△

Within each tiny person
Strikes a heart still tinier
Feebly strikes, each minute an equator
Shifts, each second
Passions pour like violent bloodied flowers
Deep from a pale and dew-wrecked face.
Ring out wild passions, striking in the foam,
Ring in sweet tenderness, lying like a foal
Caressing a soft pink small white head
As it curls in a home.

△

The world is
Playing itself over and over again in a corner of rain
Humming sadly to itself, dropping in miniature pearls
Through laces of light and fire
Spun from the sky
And stranded, floating,
It drops used on the hill
Spins the ground with cloud
Covers the sky in dull grey mourning
And moves on, still wildly caressing and moaning.

Blood! Blood! I saw the sun set draw down
Sniffing like a dog for those fine few flecks
Sitting stained red in the understairs of sky.
The magic rots and butchers, the magic rots and touches
Feebly, flaking, one pale and wild white finger
Turning through the sky, through the hours
That fly on limping blistered feet—magic
Magic came and set me on a stick, coloured
Me with the fallen rouge of many rotten rainbows,
And I stick to the stick and grin. Thin and starved
And malnutrition keeps me sticking, desperate,
A woman tortured with her children's eyes, pale as rice,
Wild with hunger, stomachs black as coal heaps
Bellying out from the sky, still smiles
To see the pale stars falling and poisoning in another's eyes.
So what? So laugh? Nothing happens, we're still
Laughing, still and laughing, beaten red against
The sun's malevolent touches burning through the heat-stung sky,
A crack of electric sparks bright and flash-blue, withers
To a sudden tree weeping in the rain, me, on my stick
Hold out pouting gloves cross-wise dripping, red,
Yellow, blind, nervously blind, the sun shouts
And blinds us, here's the blood falling through the sky
Catch a star and catch a bloody tear
Dripping from the sun's blind eye—bright,
The sun stands still at night, the night pauses
Blind and falls stock dead down like a fainting child
Dressed in black mittens, hands held to eyes,
The grave sinks, we swoon, all life is down and bleeding,
Blindness, blindness claws and catches at its eyes,
Me, here on a stick, you, crosswise and sick,
Red blue, green mind,
High bright blue blind,
Stick and sick,
Sick sick sick
Flying blind the sun bleeds
As it flies away to seek its bleeding eye,
Blood! Blood! Mud!
Stick and sick. Blood. Blood.

I have heard the stars wake in my sleep
I saw your face and heard the moons parade
Their glitter flew along a flock of sheep
And hung itself in ice upon a glade,
It hung there sparkling; all that I could do,
My love, was listening, pick it,
Pick it, think of you.

I have seen winter chuckle
And grind her teeth a powder white
That falls like dust from corpses' skulls
And fills the frost with corpses' light

Then, glittering like fools they fly
And high as swans back to the sky
I watched the snow fall, saw the rye
Grow cold and hard and stiffly lie

Like further corpses gleaming, gleaming
Empty beside the pale copse scheming
Glittering in fields, they scream and still
Breathe whiteness in, and sweetly kill.

All bastards all, and all forgotten
In long white lace, the ghosts come haunting,
The sky is white, the mirrors still
And dripping down the frosty hill

And shadows walk and shadows lurch
From out the sky back to the church
And fly the sky and seething, seething
Snow on themselves, lie breathing, breathing.

The shadows fall, the sun drops down
The sky stands still
The sun swings round
And snow, like ice, comes hard and still
And sickens deep and flies from ill
And flies to death and sings a song
The wind will drag the clouds along
The world will rock, the worlds will save
From empty cradle to empty grave.

$\triangledown$

Love is the silent flash of two hearts throbbing
As each perceives the other, faint in their distress
They shake and move in mutual painfulness,
Their aims diverge and then converge
Like fish swimming apart then making maniacal,
Like trout, for higher reaches of stream
For evil shelves throbbing with weed and leaves
Blessed and bloated, together
They silently swim their stream.

$\triangledown$

The shadowy storm that lifts its great grey wing
Flies down and chortles, murders through the night
And leaves the day to rise with rainbow stained ring
Glistening fragile over the wrecked dark blight
Of fruit ripe smashed and cutting tongues of leaves
That hang open in strips from the bright flesh of the bark
And raging whitely cling in muffled sheaves
That scatter the day's bright heapings, withered larks
Break the lull in shaggy panting breaths
That soar with the storm-toothed winds in melodies
Open and loud and flattering in their deaths'
Sweet fall the silent whistlings of the breeze,
  And as the wind with puffed out pride grows greater
  The sun's bright call of morning joys falls later.

Where is it that the moon runs
Streaming her wild white wet hair in the wind
Where I cannot pursue? Where the stars
In melting sweetness drop into lightless sweetness
Where the air disintegrates is gone
And all is clear
There will I move and mourn
At the grey ending of another's far-off sleeping.

Purple wanderings of hatred
Drag me dizzy and drenched with their heady perfume
Through the corrupt snows of magic, through wheaten passions
Tossing their heads like corn, green as morning
Comes my jealousy and sings in the air
Like a child's song, mocking itself,
Dark are my slumbers and deeper
Than dreams' deepest dreams, I dream of knives
I dream of the way I love you.

Snowflakes, icicle laces silent and shimmering through endless dull
thrush dawns,
Alive to sinking light that glitters from a mournful tree
Bowing its leaves in the wind's heavy hands. Its own dull glitter
Purpling the poppies through empty wreaths of grass,
Forcing the dead ones alive. Fresh to seed, bright at dawn
Calls birdsong, arises a river, a lake
Strewn and shorn of silver seed, beauty rests
And lies there idle, hair dressed as pondweed
Silently purple amongst the restless lake.

▽

Remembrance days, remembrance days
When all the lies are flown away
Or set in frost, I find them playing
The lies I told, you now are saying.

This is the time for writing love poetry
And this is the season of pain
This is the time when tears ramble on
Down a hedge and through the field
All silver and filled with pain,
For I have seen a face I loved
And painted it with love,
And it has pecked out all my eyes
With the tears of a paradise dove.

What happened to the ball?
It burst, it swung high as a red apple amongst the clouds
And then came careering down.

    Silence. A short moment.

And the prison?
Prison curls around me like a rat, waving its clawed great grey tail.
And the wind?
I have heard the wind whistle and move, shouting nobodies
Crying out the four wild blind corners of the earth and rising
                            through a puddle into nothing.
And then comes magic.
Magic and the earth spins.

    Silence still nothing.

Nothing moves as still as a ball
Nothing sings as grey as a prison
I have caught Nothing in the wind
And grabbed her in my breasts and sung to her

    Swinging, swinging.
The end of the world is singing
The end of the world is coming
And Nothing moves relentlessly on.

The wind mutters grey in the rain. The rat runs and people walk
like brief umbrellas clutched and busy through the orange
pavements, praying for light. Give me light and light and light.
Rinse out the sky and wash our souls in it. Stir up the earth and
drown us. The end is coming, we must be washed and prepared.

To see the world shine like a paper doll
Like a paper doll washed in satin, to feel the wind scorch
Early through the dark dews of larkspun night
Praying through lost silver fountains, bridled by the white branches
                                                        of the lilacs

Prayed on, cast out by the moon
And white footprints of worms where we walked
Laughing and talking once, the trees now cover with tall stiff pleats
Bending the sky into knots, torturing our passions
Into ideas grey as stone and hard as dust.

When the sun arises like half a green ball
Tossed and forgotten by an old tongue-torn dog,
I shall not run to catch it, nor shall I ride
Longer through the eternal pathways of night
For I have seen their satin splendour
Longer than I care to remember and I know the ways of death,
Have learned to worship the sad wildness and the grey
That bereaves in fragrant smoke from her every single breath.

Doomed conversations and sad lack-lustre deeps
Are all these ridden days drive back to me,
The carriage of oaths proudly driven through the urban streets
Wanders along mad and deserted, poppies' blood
Is spilling across the sky—I cannot bear
Her lilac truth nor the calmness of her knitting hands
As she spins her great lies
And warns us falsely, ever and again
To shoulder old burdens, finally drooping
To die.

Damnation cuts awareness like an arrow
Leaving it bleak and blind, a one-holed whirlpool
Yellow and tawny splattered against the wood
And filthy trees that grab their hands between their sides
And march, curling only their lips, their leaves
Like wild and vast mongrels praying for peace.

The dream is dead
The heart is awakened
The silver in the bull
We lie here forsaken
And listen to rain
Wringing its grey chill hands
Around us is love
Between us is banned
You know God lies there dying
Why did He say?
From the opens of darkness
Walks out the bright day,
Walks out and then vanishes.
Our lives may be saved,
We walk in our freedom
Alone to our graves.

Love is a wretched tiger tamed
With orange mildewed eye
Who runs and whimpers, locks and flames
And tries to bite the sky.

His hair is long, his locks are gold
His eyes are cold and stare
On nothing, seeing nothing
For there is nothing there.

His hooves trample deep
He prances like a cat
He laughs and cavorts and sings,
His coat is pale, he's like a rat
Who smudges the bell he swings.

Love is a wild and wonderful thing
Full of praises, full of gold
Love is a bright and glorious thing
But cold, my love, oh so cold.

Mortal monsters rise from heavy towers
And nightmares walk, thé sky is clear and fine
The dawn a rosy-handed walking child
Who crawls and stumbles on the turquoise lines
That lie from dusk to dawn,
She glittering trips
And falls in morning, laughing like an elf
With silver fingers, wiping them on clouds
She shone like you, I caught her like myself.

California is a rhyming hell
Of riches and rich blue flames
Wasted on money, spent on emotion
Wasting on and on.

California is a sweet hell
Of stolen spice kisses, moves
Behind black fences, guns and corpses
Wide blue breathless smiles.

California smiles for you,
Smile back at her,
Feel her fever
Touch her hair
Kiss her sunshine
Steal a kiss
Here on Hell's throne
Find Hell's bliss.

It's like looking at a land that has fallen asleep apart from the brief flights of insects and the unhurried stutters of the duck. The water is grey and asleep. Tossing and turning in its sleep, snoring as it raps against cold ground and dreaming somewhere out in the middle where the air, not quite so grey, rises and is lost in the trees. It is a grey silhouette of grey matter. It is an evening turntable. A bird reaches cawing across the sky and streaks in a single ski-line through the orange air. The air itself is clear and heavy resting undreaming on the tops of the trees. And lights, far away, reach out at a London that never was and never shall be again.

The sea, the sea, bring me back to the sea
To that purple blanket, cavorting and dancing over me
Running her hair through her free palms
Tossing up silver far to the palms and beyond
Bending in cool green places deep to the salad shores
That lie and wrinkle in the cold grey sun,
The stench of salt, the lie of cool free water
Fill my nose with pictures and I drown.

How can you feel so cold
When the wind blows like sunshine
Full in your face, tossing its mane
Like a timid hedgehog?

How can you feel so cold
When the lilies lie laughing
In rampant streaks of green lightning
Misted white colour,
Caught at by rainbows
And springing alive, ever-startled?

The clouds turn slowly into water
Under the pouring face of compassioned sky
That shines and reaches out in plump
Jointing fingered sun. Love waits and smiles
Gold dripping all around her, through her hair
Lie long drizzling calls of silver.
Her eyes are bright and untouched by fire
Or fear but peaceful as a hanging summer roof
On dry and blooming green. Flowers splash
In heavy tropic purples, wrinkled with the sun
Between the brows and chattering glance
At the bird-strewn air and whisper clear
   Of love's edging weak red smiles
   Slipping like harvests around them each year.

The faint fluffed edge of babies' bristling hair
Rolls like angelic mops over the fields
In cot-drawn flowers bursting from their lair
And carry-cot bars in soft beauties, it yields
Out summer in babies, dusty, hair awash
With roses, eyes soft brown and blinking
Frantic as the thrush who reaches in a rash
Of fervoured heat for the worm that's sinking
Silver beneath the singing grass that in the dark
Lilts its mourning voice to a plaintive lute
Flying round the earth from the beating lark
Who waits in bushes, yearning like a flute
    For noon and the silver ends of day
    That pretty glitter lost but will not play.

Nothing that can harm comes hatefully
It works in beauties, lifting up our eyes
To heaven's loveliness, rocking in stars
Or the ocean's deepest mists, oh to be loved
As she is, to feel your hands working on me as they do
Around her, what would I give
But my world, my life, my heart,
And—were freedom not hideous,
Is peace not hell, could truth ever be realised?
And yet, within this new-found touch of yours
I'd smell the lilies' kiss, an earwig,
A dark ugliness biting as you nibbled at my ear
And the call of a running rat within your love songs.

Light, half alive and roasted in soft, insensitive breaths
Advances slowly to prick the wounded edges of falsely staring night
And, at the turnback, flings her spear and holds
In embarrassed shock to find—empty trees and flowers and breaking
                                          up remains of stars and skies.

How is it possible to love and not be loved?
Why is your music, like music only
My soul wants to hear, rejecting all others
As the beatings of a cold wind? What is that bird
That shines around your head? That light
Spraying from your eyes straight to my heart,
What showers are these, my heart is bleating
Like a lost and woeful sheep, why when my eyes
Catch onto yours, do they startle and glow
As if aroused disastrously from sleep? God grant me death
To replace this subtle poison, love is hate,
It kills, leaving alive and strong,
Dead with passion, I bleat, loving you
Like a wail upon the hillside, voiceless
Empty-handed, I sink between your eyes
Your cruel heart like sand
Drenching on the wind.

As winter wastes into solid frozenness
The old trees bow, love on a far grey stallion
Nods and rides away, my heart is broken,
All the stars that nodded there like glittering narcissi
Have withered in the freeze, lay winter's cold hand
Cold upon my forehead, lay me out.

When the morning awakens like a fragrant child new-touched
The day ugly rears her head and stretches withered toes
Pattering on morning's pastures, we crawl like sheep
Towards mountains, nursing that huge mystery
The sky, like candles of moonlight within our breasts.

An angel with a black halo
Bending over a sports car, her silver face
Whining and sparkling with speed.
Our eyes met. Yours, like that blue
That disturbs the evening skies
Who cough and move over restfully,
Mine wide and white, the sheets of tired larks
Resting at sunrise, pale at the golden arrogant force
Of another wearing uplifted day.
This was love. The day pale and starshaped
And deliberate
As thistles dipped in moonlight.

THE RABBIT AND I $\triangledown$

Love is a slow disease that quickly spreads
Leading to fantasies, tricks of mind
Tricks of mountains and dreams and of slow moving sky.
Leading to walks along dangerous precipices
Caves full of flame
For a tiny gold handkerchief
Dragons and fairies and wizards and I
And all for a drink from a cup that is poisoned
And all for a wastrel who bought out the mountains
And all for a thing who has stolen the sky.
In poets it poisons, it rancids, it festers
It flames and it mustards, it sings out its lies
It leads them out walking
It led me out walking
It leads me out walking below sun and sky
To the dark vales of Paradise
Where shadows walk, ghosts steam
And all for a fix, a delusion, a cry
And a sob that was heard once within the mind's dream
A sob that was heard once within the mind's dream
A sob that drew pictures and coloured the sky
It drew me out screaming
For a fool who refused me
A fool who re-used me
Who would not understand me
Forever confuse me
With another, any other, what other?
A fool who took crayons and pencils at will
And drew lines on the sky –
He drew pavements, I walked them,
I wailed as I walked them,
He drew me, I drew him
With colourful eyes,
He led me out walking
Tonight in the evening
He left me, he left me in the glory of sky.
Of stars and of puddles
Of Nature, of wonder
My love like a badly cracked mirror

Reflected and cracked and suspected
A world that was not him
A world that was not me
A world that was not mine
A world that contained one thing
And one thing contained only
Me and the rabbit
And the rabbit and I.
The rabbit still stood, half shocked, half defending
Half hungry, caressing
I stared in his eye and down all around
Stood the sky and the near stars
And round all about were the mountains
In torment, and then round again
Rose the hills, sank the road
Rose the road and the grass
Where I stood
Rose up gaping and small as the sky
And the rabbit still stayed
Half possessed by a hunger
That possessed me as well
And we knew him and I
That the hunger would lessen for me
And would grow for him
Greater than sky
Greater than knowledge
Greater than anything
I would ever see
Or would sigh over
There, in his green eyes,
The hunger of heaven
His prick-lilted body like gorse upon thorn trees
A bush burned in forest, still flaming on mountains
His body a handful of grey dust and fir cones
And empty as purses all filled by the sky
He hungered, I hungered and neither drew nigh
Was this a rabbit
Or giant, that cowered
That picked and that sat and that stood
Like a pin, never moving,
I looked and I loved him
I looked, I turned from him

All round me was hunger
In his face was hunger
But no worse than mine,
For love when it bites
Is remorseless and useless
And coldly and hurtful it kisses
When you hate, it lies down in lanterns
It swears in the brakes
And it breeds in rough country
The rabbit and I
I hungry for love on a wastrel
He wasted with hunger
My love like a pocket handkerchief
His hunger like the sky
I turned, I near fainted
I walked on the ground
I crunched and I stamped
Till full of thunder the sky
Broke apart and it twisted
The rabbit still nibbled
The landshaken grass
He still paused and still stood
Like a grey pin on carpets
Carpets of glory and windy the sky
The rabbit looked and I left him
My love fraying round me
His like a beacon
And mine like a fly
The rabbit was hungry
I hungry in love
And the sound of his hunger
Was greater than mine
I walked back unsatisfied
Beaten and raving,
The poet complaining
Between land and sky
And the sun ran, the stars grew
And glittered with lightning
And so was the sky.
And the sun and the pools were all scarlet
With glittering and so was the sky
And the pools and the sun were of silver and gold
And so was the sky.

Dusk brushes her grey hair far across
Her wild and withered face, the sun sinks down
In a smother of lace and blood leaks out
Through the frost,
The air is cold
The air is dying
The faint, flawed call
Of a swallow flying.

The evening hangs like a grave dark
And overburdened with stars, they wrinkling shine
And skipping in aged brows link the moon
And fall into petty leaves of broken light
Heavens unknown, lives unspared,
Barren and criminal love is caught and bared
With silver smears, to rock in agonised shadows
High above this lofty world and bombs
Fall like flowers swiftly to bloom, destroying
Tears, smiles and empty achings of harsh bliss
That lurks lying and uncaring around the pretty stars.

What does the word unmentionable mean
A sorry shame or the skin of a dream,
Love's pale white teeth or her sharp black hair?
These things stay unmentioned anywhere.

The fields are white, the heathen walks
Throwing an orange globe the kite
High above his lakes and towers.

I saw the gold tremble ceaselessly at his ear
As he continued tossing
This was the late, cold year of his going
This was the year of his passing.

How many moons since then have shed
Their sad grey veils? Still I see within his face
The joy of all caressing
The joy and white abandon
That comes to those when playing
When playing in that garden.

Like a wrinkled paper doughnut
Thrown and sallied from wretched train windows
Came two dogs a-sniffing, like bones for cows
They fell eagerly on an orange heat, each other
Turning and whimpering for fattened female desire –
The smell of madness barking through torn leaves
Under a harsh and shredding wind. Bark! Bark!
And calls, black as cityswept roads
Roared and smelled into dusty red institutions
Blocking the sky and paying for clouds with breath
With a cry that half-smelled of anguish and half-smelled of death.

EVENING

I love you like the evening of an evening
That's still with stars and empty with desire.
Speak, broken-down, in lovely tumbling purples,
Take the rags and thirstings from this beggar mouth
Dry me out with kisses, softly
Small as rain. And the stars for my food
In dusty white tree-storms.
Lines, undissolving, and whispers
Tender of restlessness through
Snow at night.

▽

And what a night. A night full of spades
A silver night blinking at its own damnation
A night when you and I loved
And the world lay hushed and blindfolded
Deep upon us. A certain impression
Caught my attention, I felt disaster
Move her muffled hump
Straying through the weary roads of night
Our love tired and rainspotted
A slimy silver snake before its time
Let's just close our eyes
Let's just close our eyes
I just forgot myself. I felt the night
Pawing repeatedly beneath my back
I smell suspicion
I smell disaster
The breaking of a faint wine glass on the chin of our horizon
Clinks and hints at morning
A rapid fairness rises and sets
Dragging up rose petals in weary shapes of spades,
The night is heavy and smells of disaster
Your hand is wet
Your head is muffled
Your skin unset
I smell disaster.

Flapping down on the grey sunlit slumbers of the beach world, with the mocking water. It's decked with slime and curls in grey lace faintly at the edges. The park is still and empty. No one is around to shriek at the ducks who mutter their platitudes on and on into sleep. The flat pancake of water is moled by a thousand moles, scouting the surface for dirt and burying beneath. A blistering silence. A piercing silence with nothing of peace although somewhat of tranquillity. And the water curls up like a thumb around the grey concrete fingers of land.

The moon is arisen
The soft shades have strayed
And we rise from the dead
And our souls are all frayed
But still hopelessly beating
The wind tells us tales, we are saved, we are saved
Beating mass for an angel, around a mass grave,
See how the rains singing
Like moss round a stone
Like lovers round magic
The moon round a bone
Sing out hopeless and reeling
Her light shrieks of death
And the end of believing
Within day's bright breath
We'll bear you up lightly
Like stars on a flower
To the whiteness of death dew
Around your own bower.

When love is in pale slender skeleton shape
It winces and needs to fly, the air around it cannot help
And nor can the sky,
So love, in kimonos, rises and rests
In bleak kimonos of pale still fire
She sang, unstartled
Nervous but not afraid
Tempted but not persuaded
Unnoticed and still noticing.

To watch a swallow skim the air
With perfect moonlit motion betrays old passions,
They rise in curving misery
Arch across the face, a new and Viennese moon,
Then, like the swallow, like the moon,
Arch and quickly subside.

I love you like a violet dressed in misty bloom
And aching from the bite of severe spring dawns
That nag with teasing winds and frosting tempt of winter
Behind their blushing veils—life was sweet once in a song
But nags now cold and callous, hurting with blue deeps
Drowned as sea and carelessly harsh as brash autumn
Far and out wandering in a whirlwind above the seas,
Passions twist my soul on rocks and fling pebbles
Of jealousy and dirt at my eyes—I see you
With others long, blondhaired and swathed in tawny mists
Of reckless Summer, I, dark and small, alone
And ugly hang here in corners like a reckless toad
Waiting with a single undimmed brilliance
To turn in the sun and flash loud in your eye.

Let's just close our eyes
And forget the purple unwinking gleam of evening,
The early morning's white cries,
Dusk in silken glory
The world turning like a beaten clock
Close our eyes and remember
Close our eyes and forget
The red and yellow glare of fancy's strains
The disco's velvet beat under the stars' jogging feet
The end of a cloud of mushrooms
Flying apart, revealing birds
Swallows in silken arches of glory
Lording and living through the upper sky
The beach's green hope
The end of the sea and silence
Close our eyes and remember
Close our eyes and forget.

Inner tranquillity and outwardly
The seas roll back to betray a far storm
Gathering on grey beaches, lime light weary
And rolling in.

In California, the winds are blue and the sea is blue and everything is
blue, except when the sun comes out and splatters across the whole
landscape sheets and sheets of gold that tremble in the blue winds. In
California, people who have wander the streets of Los Angeles in
expensive nothing, brilliant strips and laces of bikinis and swimsuits
held together by small and so chic gold clasps, and people who
haven't wear sacks and old coats and plasters on their feet and sores
on their legs and needles in their arms and shiver in the sun that is so
cold inland because all it does is sweat on the beaches all day. In
California sex is a moving, a loving, a changing experience with men,
women, animals, children. A moving, a loving, a shifting, a
screaming and a hating. And the whole is spat on in the name of
relationships and enjoyed by the poor and rich alike. In San
Francisco, the bridges are like pieces of delicate underwear
connecting water with water and city with city. The Golden Gate is a
surprised shade of scarlet and ponderous at its own face, reclining
like a sleek and rusty alligator which, wondering at its own tolerance,
permits cars and lorries to crawl across its backbone in an endless
stream. The Bay Bridge is a mechanical fairy stretching its arms to the
sky in ungainly metal steps and writhing across the Bay in silver
dissatisfaction. California itself is a dream—beautiful and ungainly
and unexpected.

Pinkish dreams of early winter
And snow. Sleep, like a white lion
Lies smouldering, sleeping and frosted
Night's collection of tiny animals
Huddle close in the blue painted dark
And fiery animals close. This is
Shadows under a fire of white feathers and smoke,
This is the ringing and roaring of bells
Under the far, sad ocean. Open the whales,
Let the running trotters pierce the pink
Sweetness of early milk, suns' flushed rise
The end of the skies, the end of love, of the world.

The winter sky is white and still and jealous
Hanging with sullen drops of deadened leaves.
And swallows chop and change in squealing flights
Through the spinning cloud—so autumn fails
And, wounded, lies in rich red fur
Hard upon the cold-shaken ground.

Spring laughter
Summer tears
Autumn yearnings
Winter years.

As the orange still light descends naked and slumbering
The waves cantered home in a million rolling silences
Under the dark shudder of velvet trees
Shut up and resting till morning. The one-legged evening
Bowls sweetly on, around the lake, the flowers
Are green and still and grow identical to grass.

YOSEMITE

I could eat up a fly
And be swallowed by a cloud
Digested by the maw of a black dog
Who pisses down a mountainside
Like rain, pouring, slithering, like snakes
Like bears cooing in the black earth,
Frantic jays and frantic waterfalls
Flicking all together in a rock
A grey, far rock, a yellow rock
Dropping like diamonds from a diamond sky.

The earth is still and peaceful here,
It walks in silent contemplation
Wrapped in purple veils and silver clowns,
The sunlight settled sits on a rock
And sails out to sea,
The earth sits dreaming
Drenching herself in water, bathing
And endlessly scheming, scheming.

I miss Autumn and her orange hair
And her silken scarves and her rainbow veils
And her yellow feet that catch like leaves
And run like rain
From orange sails.

Great forces of destruction slow down
Desolation marches on, and the moss turns whiter
Yellow day becomes red dog.
And melts into glimmering grey
Between the silver fog.

We walked in search of natural treasure
Water and water and brides and veils
We find crowds of trees, and crowds of yellow
And crowds of people walking by

A pool of solid water lilies
Ringed with leaves and ringed with rock
A dry eye weeps, a tree grows old
And through it all a cradle rocks.

The trees are orange and golden tonight
Bright with silent burning fires, bright
And golden, yellow, flashing to the waves
And fluttering with the lilies, oh yellow, golden
Golden, yell . . . bright! bright!

A small and ugly weed
Sticks through a hole in an old grey rock

Claps in the wind and sails in the sun
And sits on its own, with its green and its brown
And its ugly face up, never looking down
At itself in the water, its ugly self,
It sits on its rock, on its dark grey shelf
Singing and crying and smiling and dying
And through it all crying "Beautiful, beautiful."

Where the puppy sits and the puppy plays
And sails with its tail through the bridal veil
As the tourists sit and the tourists chat
Of the beautiful surroundings, he's dreaming of a cat.

An arctic plant breaking into a sweat
A sheen of ivory and tightened wood
And tightened muscle glared as it stood
At the orange trees and the yellow gold
Remembering the snow where it last sold its soul.

The grass is blushing in eternal solitude
Dreamed on by the light and veils of trees
In orange yellow, cascade around the hills
Yosemite, Yosemite the old ancestor calls
The hills ring wild and gold
Around the cold lies shivering
In a clash of gold and pain.

Steep grey sheep
Mount the hills with daggers in their mouths
And poison tongues, Yosemite, Yosemite
Is calling tonight
Alone and high and wild and free
And the grass is like light
And the leaves like water
The flowers white as a cauliflower's daughter
And swaying, breathing, breezing in the wind
The wind that kills and climbs the hill
Scowling and calling for Yosemite.

An acorn squeals and curls
And turns itself into a squirrel

Fluttering, flying, dead on the breeze
A light red leaf with scruffy whisker
And fluffed out golden tail
Like a sail, an orange sail
Seafed and shipwrecked
Shipwrecked and fed by sea
With her pale green mouth
And her orange lips, and the leaf
Lies like a leaf in the pale green sea

Tufts of fringed and fronded fire
Round a dark sea, water rushes
Frantically onto its doom
Tossing its white hair sideways and back
Back to the gold at the edges
The long streaking trails of false silver
Beginning in the middle and die
The lakes grow hard and the lakes sing still
And the granite rocks boulder and clutch
Around them are fires, behind them is nothing
But the bounds of the frontiers and the quick-fire rose flush,
Behold then your beauties and star dates of morning
Behold all you golden and water's parade
How the hem of the sky dips and swirls as it curtsies
Between the bold rock shapes, the sea's like a maid
Blushing dark, blushing golden, blushing bright
Blushing free and the sound of her hair
As it rolls with the water, brings doom and destruction
On worlds faint as me.

The trees hang down browning, the lake is all stranded
The lake is all darkened, the trees made of ice
Yosemite's calling, her faint voice is falling
Through fine golden railings, through fresh golden spice
And the wine in my brain like an adder is ticking
A fresh golden adder asleep in the reeds
With the dark water rolling and soft near him strolling
Are bubbles, fresh bubbles, in silvers displayed
The moon winds out brightly, the sun sings low darkly
And fishing here lonely sit disease and death

They drink Coca-Cola, they ride on old rollers
They swing from the treetops and sing as they lessen
Diminishing, returning, the sun from the breeze
And the wind, it is bowing, the wind it is calling
Yosemite's falling in shreds to its knees.

Deadly trees with apricot leaves
And slender branches pointing the water
The water that rustles, the water that shocks
And slides along in pink rice flashes
Rest with me, oh lie with me
And the hurrying water and the apricot leaves.

Water rustles like silver and falls
Forming its own ice walls
White-spoked with pebbles and brilliantined trees
Under a pale sky, eye browed and pleased
And the water travels and frost unravels
Into knitting grey silver walls.

Purl one, knit one, purl one, knit one
The water untwines like a string of dead ice
And in it are fishes and on it a smile
That wrecks through the foam like a dead man's tongue

Keep weaving, keep wittering, keep knitting away
And do not stop heeding the blue voice of the jay
Who is calling in turquoise and blue lights together
And knits out the water like hole in a sweater.

Goodbye all the beauty, goodbye all this fall
And orange and yellow and golden and all
Man's death is a fortune, his life is a stick
That beats on disaster and shatters and sick

Goodbye all you beauties, goodbye all your friends
Who often have greeted and often have mended
I'll get you by morning, I'll wash up the shore
And I'll eat by the sea line
I'll see you no more.

Goodbye you old beauty, goodbye you old tide
Long times and I kiss you by delicate watersides
Long times in asylum, long times by the beach
And the time is all dead now, and death I cannot reach.

So we'll sing in the golden, we'll eat in the shade
We'll remember the insects, the squirrels that flame
The gold of the fire and the gold of the sea
The gold of the hillsides, the gold of the leaves
The brief gold of autumn, the bright gold of water
The long gold is foaming, the golden shore's laughter
The flight and the loneliness of old Yosemite
On her stick, on her crutches, her lost golden spice
And the trees are in winter
Our breath is in frost
Our bones are of granite
Our free hearts are lost
And blowing in winter, unbrushing the gold
That we saw blushing wild here
That caressed our soul.

We'll ride on together like stallions of ice
We'll climb up the mountains, we'll slide down the pools
We'll swing on the clouds and we'll shatter the cool
Of the new golden, fresh golden, stark golden ice.

    May God now forgive us
    With candle and leaf
    We'll leave you bright darkness
    Return to the sea

    May God now forgive us
    Light candles for mice
    Light candles for cougars
    And light up the ice

    Bereave out the dead ones
    Bereave and enroll,
    The water is withering,
    May God save my soul.

As fingers ripen bolder with the frost
And flush fair-cheeked to soft and dewy nothings
The harvest cringes blossoms soon and lost
And loses them to dowdy soft-edged doffing
Of plumes and wearing of borrowed wings
To soar like matchsticks through a broken sky
And listen to the sweet-tongued bird who sings
Of beauty's rose who'll fade and never die
And fleeing all around us, come the goats
In silver beards and great flashed drooping eye
Who skipping wildly celebrate the notes
Ascending through the bare chutes of the sky
    Until all heaven is filled with heavenly singing
    And bluebells sweeping softly cease their ringing.

L'ENNEMI   ▽

My lovely youth was a shadowed storm
Long lost and crossed and brilliantly worn
In sunshine where storms weed in ruin
And pull up flowers and fruit, they are too cruel

To me now I've reached the autumn of life
And fade with a pail and a rake
And a rasp to regrow the silence of strife
Where water runs like holes through the tombstones' sweet sake.

Who tells, who tells if flowers grown
When flooded dig their graves
And build with the seeds they sowed
The seeds that are later flooding sown

Depressed. Oh God, depression, Time eats us all
And this dark enemy devours our hearts
Our blood that we thought lost, replaces with its sickly pall
Better us, diseased us, oh better us all.

Brutal white chrysanthemums trigger the night
Into wild and gangster glories, stick-up petals
Splayed finger leaves and the bullets' red that sinks
And, shot down, blinks beneath the night's pale purple lash.

LE CORPS DE BEAUTÉ   ▽

Hand, a hand wrecked in darkest pink shells
Shadowed out in fingers, the palms blaze dark tonight
Lacing in fronds between the phantom moon's glance
Careless, full of love, see, see the blood
Dripping its melancholy red train homewards.

Let us steal and pierce these veins of silver and blue
Leading in poetry upwards, what's a crutch
To lead destroyed through arms held flapping
Like pineapples white by their sides, alabaster
Glories harsh, steers clear, the moon is white
It dies slowly in its own arms, its own sad moonlight.

Feel the trunk of this tree is hard
And grey knobbled, breasts are white and strong
Laced with fat and pricked in red needle nipples
Pointing out then down, the skin's a barrel
Of deep red wine, torn and split in the middle
On the bottom, leading to the channel of hair and blood
The cut of wildest springtime.

Stand, crouch, cripples up aloft, fill this body
This head with waxen moveable legs
Pulling from grass to wicked moon, they stretch
Like rainbows pale in bronzing glory
High to the arch of the leggy leg-ridden sky,
Stand and stand on feet who grey and flat
Like stones connect then leap from the pavement's street.

How one rises, lurching from the purple silver-starred dawn
Into the blankets of night, what is this road
So bare and lonely along which each travels
Faces cast like snails, looking for starvation
In each bleak peg of grass, arching from the roads
Long limbering legs, stretched and lying silver naked
Beside us, what have we seen in this long trek
Across the narrow blindness of roads
Looking frantic to eternity, that snails have not,
How have dreamed, wrapped in nutshells, other than them
Of flowers weird with dappled light and plunged in gold
On the tips of a petalled miser sun, tossing out
Glory in penny pinching hand above the seas
To lie in laced white blankets, spinning and foaming,
Stags prancing on water alive and free,
The gold that spins and hoops each edge
Of a poppy's finest fingertips, greeting red to orange
Snatching back, protruding like butter rams
That dip from the breath of fresh made strawberry jam,
How and where can we find in this silver misery
Surrounded pranced over by countless silver steers,
The silent path, coming from and leading to
Death behind us, and forming one long silver smear?
And in the ending, in eternity, with her sad black veil
Gaping out from the darkness of sombre night's face
Blackened into eternity, we may yet see stars
Catching the shadows that prick on our hands
And stab at our fingers lifting a veil of light
Onto Mars, on Venus, far on the feet like white sandals
Glittering in pleasures as they walk, the wildest cut
Lit and launched like a crescent moon, the body moves
A white tower through the sky, arms draped
In cotton clouds, the head, the head, the face
Falls in bowing curtains, drooped in folds of compassionate lace.

I don't need your fire
I could be contented
With skies for playthings
In the yard of my desire
Your hair like fen-leaves
Skin of disaster.

Love is a two-faced bitch who cries
Her teeth are bad and she tells you lies
She laughs and jokes and her hair is green
And her eyes are brown with a silent scream,
String her up high and swing her low
For where love goes, there will I go.

A baby laughs, a baby plays
Through tight winged tears
Through fairy days,
Oh empty fools then run and play
And skip along the sunset day.
My darling laughs and dreams and cries
And I have found night in his eyes.
I have found night and I have found frost
And everything else I found is lost.

Horror! Horror! Horror!
She sheets her white lace around my arm
And wraps it bleeding, her grey steps muffle and pause
She listens. Suddenly a bright tear
As bright as the sun's first blink upon
Tiptoed and dew-doed grass,
Hesitates, trembles and startles between lazy sheets,
She smiles a knife from out her mouth
And, raising one great hairy grey hand, lifts to my throat
Waits and plunges. The blood tastes deep,
Deep it tastes as many an emerald-starred night
Wished on by the wistless moon, endlessly circling our rancid planet
Deep as the earth's old backache, flinging up mountains
Causing rivers to bear children to the sea
Setting off the seasons like lollipops in endless flaunting
Colourful motions—summer's giddy smiles,
Spring bouncing, winter's frozen laugh
All these she sets, deeper than these
Deeper than that first strike of spliced light
Ripping through our hearts as we are born
Deader than the rest, the last cold muffled curse
Of us as we lay dying.

▽

The earth, a cold grey monster shudders and halts
Its whining wink of white flash light
Falls and stumbles, crawls up broken
Crawls on despairing, catches winds
And blows them hollow, controls the sky
To a face for tears to blow on
Blows on life and leaves it breaking.

The door beckons glistening
Dull and white-open,
I enter,—thousands of fires walking round like ants
Crowds collecting on a bush,
Christ, what was the tenth commandment
Something like fire and fear,
Could this maggot tell me? Sitting
And idly spinning, working, wreaking laces
My God, you're fat,
No, I'm not, I'm pregnant, she replied with a wink
(Ugly fat brown cow)
It's the pigment makes it plump,
Imagine, thousands of baby maggots
Running like sultry mittens everywhere
On the earth's old black branch
When we flower, when we explode,
We'll all be stars,
Walking and floating on the Universe,
Did you want to walk on water, or drown at sea?

Ga-ga-giggle. Gurgle, gurgle—oo
Pull out his dummy and give him a plum,
Can't you see the bloody apple
There it is, huge and red and glistening.
Well pick it then. Now. There.
Now what are we going to do with it?
Sell it to a snake. There aren't any.
There's one, swinging from a branch,
His skin is chequered red and black.
Did he see the blast? The mushroom's
Lovely tendrils unsnaking through the air,
God, give me air
To eat and drink and sleep on,
I'd rather starve than touch these fruits
These veg, bounties of a glorious
Giving hand—Paradise, where are you?
Give me only air to breathe on,
I'll sleep on a cloud but not amongst mushrooms'
Sickly poison—I'm sick—retching . . .
Vomit . . . yellow flowers on the sick branch

54

Here catch it! It's a cloud!
Don't you smoke yet? You will.
Pick the bloody apple.
Let's all demonstrate.
Thread me a flower, pass me a student,
Give me a pension. I'll string them
To my banner and fly them like a kite
Amongst mushrooms. Give me Art,
Give me Love, give me Life,
Didn't you know Destruction
Is here. Who cares Creation,
Creation is what signals first
Destruction is the simplest truth,
God and a judgment captures all the world's
Sweet starveling fantasies.

Pass me an air, I cannot breathe
Let alone sing, pass me a hymn,
I cannot pray,
Let alone say or stay on this foul
Maggot-ridden earth. I used to see
Swans until the mushrooms ate them,
Oh God, I love you . . . come, let's fuck.
Out, in, out, in, out in,
Exit, sweetest, buried and drowned
Smell the mushroom's sweet poisonous smell,
Your hair is ripe and ginger,
Omelette-eyes and crazy peppermint fingers,
Who needs
Or wants poetry?
Poems? Art? Love? Life?
God, leave me and take the harmony from my hair,
This dream of smell and sight and sound and visions,
Leave me the umbrella's flash
Brighter and wider than the sun,
The glowing fireball that eats all earth,
How can you fuck me
Beside this? We all wish
For loveliest, greatest things,
Suicide's the most beautiful,

The fullest, ecstatic, life and youth
Is fatal, ultimate,
Beauty and breath.
Leave me an animal,
One small grasshopper
Pleading and mowing the earth.
Tiny green wings cultivating
All that's destroyed and small green teeth
Eating it.

Since the beginning, since Light
Came calling on me here at home
Wrapped in records, sure as silk
And half as beautiful. Since Rain
The one-toed man, dragging a brief umbrella
Through dust, poured by,
I have not drunk
Nor eaten, other than of thy words,
Thou, my God, my living crucifice.

We'll love, we'll live,
We're lovely plutonium,
Eating up fireballs,
Drinking stars,
Fry me some mushrooms for this plate.
They're good for my palate.
Oh mother, mother, why did you deceive me?
Why did you bare me?
What is there in us but life,
And waiting to breathe.
Statues made of common mud and sinking in gardens
Smelling of rank compost seeds
Smeared and tossed with light
From heavenly sauces—my God,
Why hast thou . . . Why hast thou . . .
What wast thou . . . what is thou?

I see a sultana dancing with a pear
The green and the black swing merrily together
And Spring's aloft. Summer's lost.
Where's your carving knife?
We were all once cannibals   56

Beaten on an outback island
Starved on fruit. Living on air,
God, living on air. Now we cannot live,
Neither are we corpses,
Breathing stars, breathing fires
Who'd be a dragon? Who'd care?

Instinct. Instinct. Instinct.
Lift. Breathe. Out. In.
Love. Come. Come. Come.
God. Hell. Fire. Out. Out.

Women with children, eternal cradles
Flicker like candles and fall
Outside the misty night,
The poison smells and swells
It sparkles. Pretty! let me touch!
Let me kiss. If I eat apples
And breed out poison, will I too have
Face white as snow,
Cheeks bright as cherries,
Lips sweet as love-lust,
Eyes . . . eyes . . .
Brighter than the sun's dazzle blinds you,
You, my Minotaur, escape
Escape in madness to the fairies,
There, their hair is lovely white
As freshly speckled, planted corn.
God, raise the earth to beauty,
Hold off, hold off Death from me,
I'm a child, I'm a child
Not ready. Never wasted,
Why can I live without choice
And die?
Give me something to breathe.
Give me something to breathe.

Foulness, wasted and vast in smelly caverns,
Useless rhythms, stinking melodies,
Curvetting the air with beauty,

Harshness and savagery
Rest unpraised and dangerous,
Instinct loves me. Nothing does.
Alone and adrift a planet
In search of a star and finding only
Mushrooms, white and lovely-pure,
All poison's pure like sex is
Wicked easeful lusting,
Destroyed by those who sex it
Who are you? Who are you anyway?
What right did you have
To lead me, to take me in here,
To destroy me? Oh stink, stink.
Stickbeaks, wasted,
Shrivelled feathers
Flaming, flaming, flaming,
Life in lust and ashes,
Everything here is shrivelled.
The snake has shed his skin,
The branch its dust,
We are alone here with this geranium
Growing into a mushroom,
Nature, how lovely,
You are. Oh Roi, of all hearts
Roi of mine, eating and pecking like swans
What was that ugliness you hid
And called soul? Why did you not care?
Does no-one care? Not anywhere?
Give me something to breathe.
I love you. Failing energy
Resting through the stars.

The air is shimmering harsh tonight,
Trees prick like fingers, the grass
Waves its coats at the passing fauns
And flowers, all is silent. Institutions
Breathe and breed. There, in distance,
A factory chimney, the broken back
Of a mine. Unemployed and useless.
Build, build, build, uplift

And create all uplifting,
God, give me divine power
To recreate a single swallow
Breathing in the morning,
Or a leaf, with edges faintly withered
Golden, no silver's here,
The fire's rusted.
Slowly a smooth smell, empty smoke
Arrives from the ancient smell,
Mushrooms dance, wreaths
Lift the sky and redden and darken
Like poppies. Look at this picture of a bomb
Where am I? Is this hell
Or heaven, will someone, Christ,
Let me know. Oh bomb
Bomb, I worship you, idol of the great,
Your loveliness eclipses and statues
All others. Your lovely single eye
Burning the trees and shooting the sky
Who staggers and falls, who else,
Makes the Universe, but you? Bomb,
For this idyll will you not give me
Some breath, some sight of cursory wastes
On which I loved to look, a faint
And ugly dimhearted green where suns
Shone and sang. Inside my skin
I feel your love prickle and burn,
Let us fuck, here, on the destruction
Of this simple world, trembling
Like a shy unnoticed jewel in
Heaven's scratching ear. Reached and
Plucked, my single flower,
White and ugly. No gold or silver,
Jewels or pearls but earth
Like dirt and feeble glittering flowers,
Wrecked by God and man,
Empty withered sands. Hopeless
Useless defenceless lives.
God, I loved you.

Watch this bomb dance,
His silver fingers playing on the clouds
Twisting and shrivelling them to
Burning, flaking mushrooms,
One side flies you up
The other flies you down,
Which side will you take, my love
For I will take the same,
Oh no, we can't, each
Must come to God on his own,
Leave me now and pray,
I'll watch you fly away in the blast.

Radium, my love, you breathe fire
Plutonium love and ancient
Dreams of savage wisdom,
Roi, come to me now, here
On this tip of a perished world,
Flickered and empty wasted
Useless cries for help.
Come to me baby, dance, here
Bare your baby teeth,
Lift your darling mouth,
Let me suckle you here
At the feet of the bomb. Bow,
Bow, baby and worship
Your death, drink this water,
Move the frog that's lying dead in it,
We'll eat him too.
But separately. One must keep
Decency in death. Stay alone.
Here love, there's no milk
The mushrooms drank it,
God was thirsty, my love,
Flew up in a cloud and vanished.
Life is lonely baby. Fall-out
Keep out, we are lucky,
Lucky. Lucky. Luck.
I've heard the sea is green now.
I can't, I can't,
Why am I writing this?
Why do I not die?
Like those others who cared
And loved and lost,

What? What?
Leave me breath in your will,
The world is black,
The world is burning,
Cuddle close, my baby,
Suckle this burning wasted breast
Pray to the mushrooms for death,
Cry and grimace out breath,
Leave me the world,
Leave the world
In your will.
Oh Roi, I loved you,
Why have you flown,
Where is the life you took?
Naked and soulless
Stroll amongst the apes,
Kiss heaven and sink and die,
Ah darling, spreading like a cancered
Snake on rotten.
And you, my God, my earth, my world,
My life, my love. What of you?
Living in highest
In gold above us.
Breathing above us,
We, the dead, the shattered,
The mushroom-killed,
Hopeless poets, hopeless cries,
Faintly hearted breaths
Catch us no longer,
We, the ghosts of a fire
Stark on the hideous earth,
Bombs brighter than the sun,
Lovelier than fire,
Wider than love
Better than creation,
Oh earth, miserable loveless child
Beaten and starved, careless
And flouted, useless ugly
Plough-ridden peaceless,
Frantic, hopeless,
Lined and wrinkled childish
Ugly, foul and stinking
Unweeded, gross, grossest
Of all, lustful,
Natural wonderful earth. I love you.

You flirt and frown
And dirt and drown
And I, here, jealous
Hate you with relish
And love you with silk
And beggar's milk.

Eyes, ripe as peppermints
Blinking in a white sky,
Lips, lips sweet as love-nuts
Tongue salt as the sea
And deeper, love, how I love you,
Your eyes are bluer than the sunset's haystack
Clotted against the sky,
Lips, sweet as love,
Lips sweet as . . . lips sweet as love-nuts.

Close your sleep-trimmed eyes, my love
I'll bring for you a trembling dove
That you can kill or you can shove
In cruel pain back at the skies.

Above us lie the wrecks of men
The bleak skies are black
And crow wings nestle, moving like tractors
Through the cold bleak whinings of the air

How the snow is fair
How our lives are still
Come to me my love
And let me kill you

Your eyes like stones
Your teeth like milk
You feel as soft
As soft as silken worms
Crawling underground

Leave me now!
Desert the ground.
Desert the air
A silver train is coming down
Is slowly descending through the air.

Frost sparkles and our hands are released
Give me your hand, we'll both pray for peace.

When I was a child, I watched the light birds fly
And dreamed of killing, kissing their cold dead eyes
And burying bodies deep in the sweet earth
Then, I remember thinking as I watched, then they could no longer
fly.

Now I'm not a child
And so I do not watch birds fly nor do I kill them.
Instead I watch dreams fly
Dreams flying like birds
Against a harsh and adult sky
And, because I'm bigger now, I can reach
I can touch the whole length of sky
I can catch my own dreams
And because I'm an adult now
I can pull them down crying beside me
And slowly and sweetly strangle them
And kiss them as they grow cold
And bury them in hallowed ground
And wait for them to die,
I know now that the birds did not matter
It was only the dreams that I wanted to die.